THE LITTLE BOOK OF
SURVIVING
MOTHERHOOD

Published in 2024 by OH!
An Imprint of Welbeck Non-Fiction Limited,
part of Welbeck Publishing Group.
Offices in: London – 20 Mortimer Street, London W1T 3JW
and Sydney – Level 17, 207 Kent St, Sydney NSW 2000 Australia
www.welbeckpublishing.com

ISBN 978-1-80069-567-2

Compiled and written by: Victoria Denne
Editorial: Tanisha Ali
Project manager: Russell Porter
Design: Tony Seddon
Production: Jess Brisley

A CIP catalogue record for this book is available from the British Library

Printed in China

10 9 8 7 6 5 4 3 2 1

THE LITTLE BOOK OF
SURVIVING
MOTHERHOOD

A MODERN MOTHER'S
HANDBOOK

CONTENTS

INTRODUCTION

Everyone says having children is life-changing, but you don't *really* believe them—not, that is, until you hold your newborn baby in your arms, feel that unconditional and all-encompassing love for your little one, or find yourself binge-watching *Bluey* episodes with your toddler at 5am on a Wednesday morning eating Cheerios straight from the box.

As a mom, you start work from the moment you open your eyes and don't stop until the second your head hits the pillow at night. There are no vacationss, no wages, and your boss—at least until they go to school—is at best unreasonable, at worst tyrannical. And then, just when you thought you were getting good at this parenting lark, they become teenagers...

No matter how old your kids are, there's no doubt about it; being a mother is one of the most demanding, fulfilling, not to mention downright *hardest* jobs in the world, full of soaring highs, crushing lows and veritable *mountains* of laundry. As well as the demands of the job itself, there's also the added pressure that society puts on mothers to be the "perfect mom" (whatever that means), not to mention somehow managing to "have it all"—kids, partner, career, and an Instagram-worthy house to boot. No wonder moms are exhausted.

Whether you're currently expecting, or your little one has just arrived and you're wondering if you'll ever sleep or wear clean clothes again, if you're in the thick of parenting or sending them off into the world as (almost) proper adults, this book has got you covered. In it you'll find precisely none of the answers and all of the encouragement, with words of wisdom, humour and reassurance from parents who've done it and got the (vomit-covered) T-shirt to prove it, as well as some fun facts about motherhood to keep your mind occupied during those 2am feeds—or while you're *definitely watching* them go down the slide for the millionth time...

Because while motherhood is undoubtedly special, it's not without its challenges... and anyone who says otherwise is either a saint, or has a *really* good nanny.

CHAPTER
ONE

Oh Baby Baby

Becoming a mother is a life-changing event, and those first few months with a newborn can be the most joyous—and the most demanding.

Whether your pregnancy was meticulously planned, medically coaxed, or happened by surprise, one thing is certain— your life will never be the same.

Catherine Jones

66

Making the decision
to have a child—it's
momentous.
It is to decide forever
to have your heart
go walking around
outside your body.

Elizabeth Stone

Ancient deities associated with childbirth include Eileithyia, the Greek goddess of childbirth; the ancient Egyptian goddess Hathor, associated with fertility and motherhood; and Frigg, the Norse goddess who was said to watch over married and labouring women.

Livescience.com

"

Maternity leave is the most busy-bored, happy-sad you'll ever be, whilst also the most tired you've ever been. It's like the farthest thing from a vacation and the closest thing to a mental breakdown. IDK how else to describe it. It's a weird time.

"

@mybestmomfriend

66

No one told me I
would be coming home
in diapers, too.

99

Chrissy Teigen

According to the *Journal of Pediatrics*, Danish, German and Japanese babies cry the least, while British, Canadian and Italian babies cry the most.

The Guardian

A sleeping baby is the new happy hour.

Being a mom has
made me so tired.
And so happy.

Tina Fey

The most popular month
for having babies in the US
is August, and Tuesday
is the day of the week on
which most babies are born.

Factretriever.com

66

There was never a
child so lovely, but his
mother was glad to get
him to sleep.

99

Ralph Waldo Emerson

"Mummy Brain"—the brain fog that is widely reported to go hand in hand with pregnancy and new motherhood—is very real and is due to the fact that a woman's brain physically changes during this time.

Livescience.com

"

A baby will make love
stronger, days shorter,
nights longer, bankroll
smaller, home happier,
clothes shabbier, the
past forgotten, and the
future worth living for.

Unknown

353,000 babies are born every day; that's 255 births each minute.

EngageEmployee.com

"

Sleep, at this point,
is just a concept,
something I'm looking
forward to investigating
in the future.

"

Amy Poehler

> 66
>
> I've learned that it's way harder to be a baby. For instance, I haven't thrown up since the '90s and she's thrown up twice since we started this interview.
>
> 99
>
> **Eva Mendes**

"

I don't want
to sleep like a baby.
I want to sleep like
my husband.

"

Unknown

"

A toy Tamagotchi is
more communicative
than a human baby,
OK? Because the toy
will at least tell you
when it poos.

"

Ali Wong

By the time her baby
reaches the age of two, the
average mother will have
changed approximately
7,300 nappies.

Haba.com

66

Be patient with
yourself. You and your
baby are both learning
new things each day.

99

Unknown

"

No one is ever quite ready;
everyone is always caught off guard.
Parenthood chooses you. And you
open your eyes, look at what you've
got, say 'Oh, my gosh,' and recognize
that of all the balls there ever were,
this is the one you should not drop.
It's not a question of choice.

"

Marisa de Los Santos

Having a baby is just living
in the constant unexpected,
you never know when
you're gonna get crapped
on, or when you're gonna
get a big smile or when that
smile immediately turns into
hysterics.

Blake Lively

You might name your baby, but they also name you. The "ma" sound is typically the first sound a baby vocalizes, and almost every language has used this as the root of their word for "mother".

Livescience.com

66

Having children just
puts the whole world
into perspective.
Everything else just
disappears.

99

Kate Winslet

Becoming a mother
makes you realize you
can do almost anything
one-handed.

Unknown

33

On average, it takes a mom
2 minutes and 5 seconds
to change a nappy, which
is equivalent to about two
40-hour working weeks
each year.

Factretriever.com

"

Having a child is like getting a tattoo... on your face. You better be committed.

"

Elizabeth Gilber

"

Twelve years later, the memories of those nights, of that sleep deprivation, still make me rock back and forth a little bit. You want to torture someone? Hand them an adorable baby they love, who doesn't sleep.

"

Shonda Rhimes

Top 10 Countries for Maternity Leave

Estonia —62 weeks
Croatia —58 weeks
Bulgaria —58 weeks
UK —52 weeks
Bosnia and Herzegovina —52 weeks
Montenegro —52 weeks
Albania —52 weeks
Ireland —42 weeks
Macedonia —39 weeks
Norway —35+ weeks

66

Ah, babies. They're more than just adorable little creatures on whom you can blame your farts.

99

Tina Fey

66

My biggest parenting
conundrum: why is it
so hard to put someone
who is already sleepy
to sleep?

99

Chrissy Teigen

CHAPTER
TWO

Raising Little Humans

Just when you thought it couldn't get harder, they walk, and talk, and then talk back...

Silence is golden. Unless you have kids. Then silence is just suspicious.

"

A two-year-old is kind of like having a blender, but you don't have a top for it.

"

Jerry Seinfeld

Toddler to-do list

1. Ask for waffle.

2. Refuse waffle.

3. Ask why your waffle was taken away.

4. Cry because you don't have your waffle.

66

Cleaning your house
while your kids are
still growing is like
shovelling the walk
before it stops snowing.

99

Phyllis Diller

There are around 2 billion mothers in the world.

66

Having children is
like living in a frat
house: nobody sleeps,
everything is broken,
and there's a lot of
throwing up.

99

Ray Romano

"

A mother is never needed more than when she's in the shower, going to the bathroom, or about to eat something.

"

Unknown

"

It just occurred to me
that the majority of
my diet is made up
of food that my kid
didn't finish...

"

Carrie Underwood

"

I used to give my
friends who have kids
advice all the time,
and they would look
at me like I had three
heads. And then, when
I had two, I literally
apologized to all my
friends.

"

Jennifer Lopez

Instead of tucking them in bed nice and early, Spanish parents typically keep their kids up until around 10pm so they can learn how to socialize with other members of the family.

90% of parenting is just thinking about when you can lie down again.

"

I always say, 'If you
aren't yelling at
your kids, you're not
spending enough
time with them.'

"

Reese Witherspoon

"

When my kids become
wild and unruly, I use
a nice, safe playpen.
When they're finished,
I climb out.

"

Erma Bombeck

66

Not all who wander
are lost. Some are just
moms. In Target. Hiding
from their children.

99

@jocieopc

Think one is too many?

The mother with the most children is Mrs Feodor Vassilyev of Russia, who gave birth to 69 kids between 1725 and 1765.

Factretriever.com

66

Why don't kids understand that their nap is not for them but for us?

99

Alyson Hannigan

66

Sweater, *n*.: garment
worn by child
when its mother is
feeling chilly.

99

Ambrose Bierce

"

Every day, when you're raising kids, you feel like you could cry or crack up and just scream 'This is ridiculous!' because there's so much nonsense, whether it's what they're saying to you or the fact that there's avocado or poop on every surface.

"

Kristen Bell

"

Asked to switch seats on the plane because I was sitting next to a crying baby. Apparently, that's not allowed if the baby is yours.

"

@mommyshorts

"

[Having four kids is] endless stuff. It's endless entertainment, it's endless stress, endless responsibility. Everyone's at different ages and levels, everyone's into different stuff. But everyone is into slime.

"

Maya Rudolph

"

Usually the triumph of my day is, you know, everybody making it to the potty.

"

Julia Roberts

As of 2023, the average cost of raising a child (to 18) in the UK is £202,660. That's about 11,250 a year, or 938 a month.

The Times

66

Children are like crazy, drunken small people in your house.

Julie Bowen

"

I don't care how cute your kid is. When you wake up in the middle of the night and see them standing next to your bed, they are terrifying.

"

@maughammom

"

Becoming a mom to me means that you have accepted that for the next 16 years of your life, you will have a sticky purse.

"

Nia Vardalos

In the Talmud, parents are instructed to teach their children to swim — likely a metaphor for encouraging independence.

"

When I tell my kids I'll do something in a minute, what I'm really saying is 'Please forget.'

"

@SarcasticMommy4

Recipe for Iced Coffee

1. Have kids.
2. Make coffee.
3. Forget you made coffee.
4. Drink it cold.

@toni_hammer

CHAPTER
THREE

The Perfect Mom Myth

If there's one thing every mom should know, it's that, contrary to popular opinion, there is no such thing as a *perfect mother*.

❝

There's no way to
be a perfect mother
and a million ways
to be a good one.

❞

Jill Churchill

"

The fastest way to break the cycle of perfectionism and become a fearless mother is to give up the idea of doing it perfectly—indeed to embrace uncertainty and imperfection.

"

Arianna Huffington

People don't really talk honestly about how difficult being a mom actually is and what things we sacrifice every day in order to be good moms.

Jenni Ogden

Things No One Tells You About Being a Mom #1

You will wonder whether you're cut out for this at least 50 times a day.

66

You're always going to wonder if you're doing things wrong, but that's what it means to be a mom, to care so much about someone else that you just want to be as perfect as possible.

Naya Rivera

66

I think the hardest part about being a mother is just knowing that you're never enough. No matter how many books you read, no matter how many toys your kids have or schedules they follow... you will never be able to do it all perfectly.

Jessica Alba

Things No One Tells You About Being a Mom #2

For better or worse, you will at some point channel your own parents.

Motherhood is a choice you make every day, to put someone else's happiness and well-being ahead of your own, to teach the hard lessons, to do the right thing even when you're not sure what the right thing is... and to forgive yourself, over and over again, for doing everything wrong.

Donna Ball

"Mom" Around the World

Mandarin Chinese: **Māma**
Hindustani: **Māṃ**
Spanish: **Madre** or **mama**
Arabic: **Māma**
Malay: **Ibu**
Portuguese: **Mãe**
French: **Mère**
Punjabi: **Māṁ**
German: **Mutter**
Swedish: **Mor**
Korean: **Eomeoni**
Tamil: **Am'mā**

Things No One Tells You About Being a Mom #3

Nothing will embarrass you anymore. (With the possible exception of toddler tantrums in the supermarket.)

"

You are exactly the
mother your child
needs. Knowing that
will change your
entire perspective.

"

Lauren Tingley

66

I'd love to be a Pinterest mom. But it turns out I'm more of an Amazon Prime mom.

99

Unknown

66

There are so many
times you will feel
you have failed, but
in the eyes, heart and
mind of your child,
you are supermom.

99

Stephanie Precourt

Things No One Tells You About Being a Mom #4

You will laugh more tears of joy—and frustration—than you ever thought possible.

"

You can be a mess
and still be a good
mom. We are allowed
to be both.

"

@katiebinghamsmith

"

Being a mother isn't easy. And being able to admit your weakness as a parent is one of the most important things you'll ever do for your child.

"

Katrina Alcorn

"

What being a parent doesn't require is being perfect.

"

Anna Quindlen

66

If you're completely
exhausted and don't
know how you're
going to keep giving
this much of yourself
day after day, you're
probably a good parent.

Bunmi Laditan

Things No One Tells You About Being a Mom #5

The back seat of your car will—I repeat, *will*—become the most disgusting place on Earth.

66

We're all imperfect
parents, and that's
perfectly okay.
Tiny humans need
connection, not
perfection.

L. R. Knost

"

Breathe. The moments
matter. Not the perfect ones,
but every single day, nitty-
gritty, showing-up moments
of motherhood. Your kids
don't need perfection, just
you. Showing up, loving,
giving and trying, and
simply being their mom.

"

Rachel Marie Martin

"

I think being a mom is the hardest job in the world. I don't know how women do it without going crazy.

"

Britney Spears

Things No One Tells You About Being a Mom #6

Parenting can be lonely.
Get help whenever you can.

66

Parenting shouldn't feel like a
competitive sport. It's plenty
challenging without any added
obstacles. Strive to be loving and
kind; have the courage to ask for
help, take a break when you need it,
celebrate all the great stuff, be kind
to yourself, and be yourself. That's
who your kid loves anyways.

99

Ariadne Brill

"

Parenting is f***ing hard.

"

Adele

"
There is no such thing as a perfect parent. So, just be a real one.
"

Sue Atkins

Behind every great child is a mom who's pretty sure she's screwing it all up.

66

What good mothers
and fathers instinctively
feel like doing for their
babies is usually best
after all.

99

Benjamin Spock

66

Parenting is a lifetime job and does not stop when a child grows up.

99

Jake Slope

66

Children start out loving
their parents, but as they
grow older and discover their
parents are human, they
become judgmental. And
sometimes, when they mature,
they forgive their parents,
especially when they discover
they are also human.

Oscar Wilde

CHAPTER

FOUR

Parenting Hacks

When it comes to raising kids, the only thing we need more than help is to know that we're not alone on this crazy journey.

So, here are some top parenting tips from those right there in the trenches with you...

> **"**
> The easiest way
> to shop with kids is
> not to.
> **"**

@relaxingmommy

"

A good way to prepare
yourself for parenting
is to talk to rocks
because they have
similar listening habits.

"

Unknown

"

The quickest way for a
parent to get a child's
attention is to sit down
and look comfortable.

"

Lane Olinghouse

Mumsnet.com Decoded—Part 1

For when you inevitably find yourself down a rabbit hole at 3am...

BC: Before children
BF: Breastfeeding
BFP: Big fat positive (referring to a pregnancy test)
BLW: Baby-led weaning
CC: Controlled crying
DD: Darling/dear daughter
DC: Darling/dear child

"

When your children
are teenagers, it's
important to have a
dog so that someone
in the house is happy
to see you.

"

Nora Ephron

"

If your kids are giving
you a headache, follow
the directions on the
aspirin bottle, especially
the part that says keep
away from children.

"

Susan Savannah

"

Like all parents, my husband and I just do the best we can, and hold our breath, and hope we've set aside enough money to pay for our kids' therapy.

Michelle Pfeiffer

The greatest gift a parent can give a child is self-confidence.

Stewart Stafford

66

Try waking up an
hour earlier every
day, so you can be
15 minutes late instead
of 30 minutes late.

99

Unknown

66

The Golden Rule of
Parenting is do unto
your children as you
wish your parents had
done unto you!

99

Louise Hart

"

Don't worry that children never listen to you; worry that they are always watching you.

"

Robert Fulghum

Mumsnet.com Decoded—Part 2

DH: Darling/dear husband
DS: Darling/dear son
EBF: Exclusively breastfeeding
FF: Formula-feeding
HTH: Hope this helps
IIRC: If I remember correctly
IMHO: In my humble opinion

"

Clean the house for 2 hours. Watch the humans you created destroy it in 10 minutes. Repeat for 20 years. This is parenthood.

Unknown

"

The point of parenting is not to have all the answers before we start out, but instead to figure it out on the go as our children grow. Because as they do, so will we.

"

Bridgett Miller

66

Being a parent is like folding a fitted sheet; no one really knows how.

99

Unknown

Mumsnet.com Decoded—Part 3

JFGI: Just f**king Google it
MC: Miscarriage
OH: Other half
OTOH: On the other hand
PFB: Precious first born
PG: Pregnant
PITA: Pain in the a**e

66

Parenting is yelling 'you just had a snack!' over and over until you give in and throw them another snack.

99

@loud_momma

"

Parenthood... It's
about guiding the
next generation, and
forgiving the last.

"

Peter Krause

66

If you have never been hated by your child, you have never been a parent.

99

Bette Davis

Mumsnet.com Decoded—Part 4

RL: Real life
SAHM: Stay at home mother
SIOB: Sharp intake of breath
TIA: Thanks in advance
TTC: Trying to conceive
WAHM: Working at home mother
WWYD: What would you do

66

The truth is, parenting as well as we can is always hard—really, truly, the hardest thing any of us has ever done.

99

Laura Markham

"

The hardest part
of being a mom?
Letting go.

"

Mandy Hale

"

No parent is always conscious, gentle, positive, peaceful, and authentic. We have to choose to be and practice moment by moment, day after day. The more we practice, the stronger we grow.

"

Lelia Schott

66

I want my children to have all the things I couldn't afford. Then I want to move in with them.

99

Phyllis Diller

> **"**
>
> # Parenting was much easier when I was raising my non-existent kids hypothetically.
>
> **"**

Unknown

Parenting hack

There are no hacks.
Everything is hard. These
kids don't listen. This is your
life now. Godspeed.

CHAPTER
FIVE

The Joys of Motherhood

As a concept, it's hard to adequately define. Even so, here we celebrate all things "mother"—the good, the bad and the even better.

113 million Mothers' Day cards are exchanged annually in the USA.

66

A mother need only step
into the shower to be
instantly reassured she
is indispensable to every
member of her family.

99

Lynne Williams

66

Motherhood is basically finding activities for children in three-hour pockets of time for the rest of your life.

99

Mindy Kaling

Motherhood: feeding
them as a baby and
then through most of
their twenties.

Unknown

"

When you are a mother, you are never really alone in your thoughts. A mother always has to think twice, once for herself and once for her child.

Sophia Loren

"

Motherhood is tough.
If you just want
a wonderful little
creature to love, you
can get a puppy.

"

Barbara Walters

Life doesn't come with a manual, it comes with a mother.

66

A mother
understands what a
child does not say.

99

Jewish proverb

"

The art of mothering is to teach the art of living to children.

"

Elaine Heffner

"

[Motherhood is] the biggest gamble in the world. It is the glorious lifeforce. It's huge and scary—it's an act of infinite optimism.

Gilda Radner

"

Motherhood is wonderful,
but it's also hard work. It's
the logistics more than
anything. You discover you
have reserves of energy you
didn't know you had.

"

Deborah Mailman

Mother Earth, or Gaia, was the first goddess in Greek mythology. Once she had created herself out of primordial chaos, she created the Earth and the rest of the universe.

"

Motherhood has relaxed me in many ways. You learn to deal with crisis. I've become a juggler, I suppose. It's all a big circus, and nobody who knows me believes I can manage, but sometimes I do.

"

Jane Seymour

66
Motherhood is an extreme sport. That's why we have to wear exercise clothes every day.

99

Unknown

"

All mothers are working mothers.

"

Unknown

"

A vacation frequently
means that the family
goes away for a rest,
accompanied by
mother, who sees that
the others get it.

"

Marcelene Cox

66

Biology is the least of what makes someone a mother.

99

Oprah Winfrey

In an early precursor to Mothers' Day, the ancient Greeks would hold festivals to celebrate mother goddesses Rhea and Cybele.

❝

Motherhood was the great equalizer for me; I started to identify with everybody.

❞

Annie Lennox

"

A suburban mother's role is to deliver children; obstetrically once and by car forever after.

"

Peter De Vries

Although nameless, one of the most famous literary mothers is Grendel's mother from *Beowulf*.

She attacks an army to avenge the death of her son.

66

Mother is a verb. It's
something you do. Not
just who you are.

99

Cheryl Lacey Donovan

"

Motherhood has taught me the meaning of living in the moment and being at peace. Children don't think about yesterday, and they don't think about tomorrow. They just exist in the moment.

"

Jessalyn Gilsig

> ❝
>
> Motherhood is not
> for the faint-hearted.
> Frogs, skinned knees,
> and the insults of
> teenage girls are not
> meant for the wimpy.
>
> ❞

Danielle Steel

The sound of their mother's voice lowers a child's levels of cortisol, the stress hormone, and increases their level of oxytocin, the "love" hormone.

Habausa.com

66

When you are looking at your mother, you are looking at the purest love you will ever know.

99

Charley Benetto

Motherhood is a constant learning process that requires flexibility and a sense of humour. And just when you think you have it all figured out, your children like to remind you that you certainly don't.

Stacey A. Shannon

During pregnancy,
mothers exchange cells
with their children
through the placenta.
These cells can live on in
the mother for years.

Livescience.com

66

A mother is a person who, seeing there are only four pieces of pie for five people, promptly announces she never did care for pie.

99

Tenneva Jordan

❝

I like to think of motherhood
as a great big adventure.
You set off on a journey,
you don't really know how
to navigate things, and you
don't exactly know where
you're going or how you're
going to get there.

Cynthia Rowley

"

Grown doesn't mean
nothing to a mother.
A child is a child.
They get bigger, older,
but grown. In my heart
it don't mean a thing.

"

Toni Morrison

66

The influence of a
mother in the lives of
her children is beyond
calculation.

99

James E. Faust

66

A mother is not a person to lean on, but a person to make leaning unnecessary.

99

Dorothy Canfield Fisher

66

A mother's love liberates.

99

Maya Angelou

"

Mothers can forgive anything! Tell me all, and be sure that I will never let you go, though the whole world should turn from you.

"

Louisa May Alcott

"

No matter how old a
mother is, she watches
her middle-aged
children for signs of
improvement.

"

Florida Scott-Maxwell

"

The only love that
I really believe in is
a mother's love for
her children.

"

Karl Lagerfeld

66

Motherhood is the greatest thing and the hardest thing.

99

Ricki Lake

CHAPTER
SIX

You Got This, Mama

When you're feeling lost or overwhelmed, overstimulated or at breaking point, let these words of wisdom inspire you to keep going.

"

The days are long but the years are short.

"

Gretchen Rubin

"

If you're worried
about being a good
mother, it means you
already are one.

"

Unknown

"

Enjoy the little
things, for one day
you may look back
and realize they were
the big things.

"

Robert Brault

"

Having kids—the
responsibility of rearing
good, kind, ethical,
responsible human
beings—is the biggest job
anyone can embark on.

"

Maria Shriver

❝

A mother's love for her child is like nothing else in the world. It knows no law, no pity, it dates all things and crushes down remorselessly all that stands in its path.

❞

Agatha Christie

"

Sometimes being a parent is like being shot at. You don't know if you can make it to the end of the day without getting hit... but somehow we do—and when we arrive in this world where everyone needs us so much, what happens? We feel alive!

"

Jodi Picoult

"

Youth fades; love
droops; the leaves
of friendship fall; a
mother's secret hope
outlives them all.

"

Oliver Wendell Holmes

Children are not a distraction from more important work. They are the most important work.

C. S. Lewis

"

Hugs can do great amounts of good—especially for children.

"

Princess Diana

"

While we try to teach
our children all about
life, they teach us what
life is all about.

"

Angela Schwindt

> **A mother's love endures through all.**

Washington Irving

❝

You will never really know what
kind of parent you were or if you
did it right or wrong. Never. And
you will worry about this and them
as long as you live. But when your
children have children, and you
watch them do what they do, you
will have part of an answer.

❞

Robert Fulghum

"

Being a mom is being
the bravest person
you know. It's being
unapologetically who
you are even when it
scares everyone else
around you.

"

Emily Henderson

66

Women do not have to sacrifice personhood if they are mothers. They do not have to sacrifice motherhood in order to be persons. Liberation was meant to expand women's opportunities, not to limit them. The self-esteem that has been found in new pursuits can also be found in mothering.

99

Elaine Heffner

"

Live in the moment and make it so beautiful that it will be worth remembering.

"

Fanny Crosby

Kids don't stay with you if you do it right. It's the one job where the better you are, the more surely you won't be needed in the long run.

Barbara Kingsolver

"

A mother is she who can take the place of all others but whose place no one else can take.

"

Cardinal Mermillod

"

It's not what you do for
your children but what
you have taught them
to do for themselves
that will make them
successful human beings.

Ann Landers

"

Sometimes the strength of motherhood is greater than natural laws.

"

Barbara Kingsolver

"
I know how to do
anything—I'm a mom.
"

Roseanne Barr

❝

Being a mom isn't easy... But being able to look at your kids and say, 'I did that! I made them!' is pretty freaking amazing.

❞

Alyssa Milano